Trust
Fall

William Gee

Out-Spoken Press
London

Published by Out-Spoken Press,
Unit 39, Containerville
1 Emma Street
London, E2 9FP

All rights reserved
© William Gee

The rights of William Gee to be identified as the author of this work have been asserted by them in accordance with section 77 of the Copyright, Designs and Patents Act 1988.

A CIP record for this title is available from the British Library.

This book is in copyright. Subject to statutory exception and to provisions of relevant collective licensing agreements, no reproduction of any part may take place without the written permission of Out-Spoken Press.

First edition published 2023
ISBN: 978-1-7399021-7-9

Typeset in Adobe Caslon
Design by Patricia Ferguson
Printed and bound by Print Resources

Out-Spoken Press is supported using public funding by the National Lottery through Arts Council England.

'What a terrible life, I think now, to have to move so fast just to stay in one place.'

— Ocean Vuong

'Bad luck, loss, pain. If you make something out of it, then you've no longer been bested by these events'

— Louise Glück

Contents

26	1
sickness eats up every space for you	2
fog (one)	3
migration	4
until necessary open arms	5
history repeats itself	6
being here is less and less ok	7
what's wrong with me	8
11"11	9
fog (two)	10
w/	11
the apples	12
this morning	13
ulcer	14
fog (nine)	15
under	16
remote	17
soho square	18
Acknowledgements	21

26

lilies bowing heavy through the heatwave
sweat gathered in the lint tray I am trying hard to leave
my flat   to practice a tenderness that doesn't end
all the time in my bathroom

  dark blue exhaustion
hanging bags above my cheeks
    dropping my jeans to my ankles

walking myself back up the high street
I am letting go

of counting steps   kicking gum loose from cracks
   I must not tread on

I am making this please don't die
this please calm down
so little
against the long slap of this
     reduced mobility
           blown out belly
    an eye for clean and quiet bathrooms
in each hot corner of this big city I want

sickness eats up every space for you

in some parts of this city you
the air that struggles through your chest
the way I could hold you right now but I haven't

instead in the low hope of a sunday ending
a young man faints in our bathroom
head narrowly missing the cabinet thank god

but now we're both approximating
the volume of red that is not soaking our carpet
the deep blue his shinbone is riddled with

in the morning you poach eggs for his body
spinach to bring up his iron and I sit
inside of him like a church

thank god you still love me but how
between the thin peace of night and working day

pepper in our back teeth
crumbs in the butter
the horrible thud of how heavy I'm getting

fog (one)

time   measured & ignored
   presses

my palms   against my temples
for light relief to this fresh migraine

I am lying in
a sweat stain the shape of my body

these days since I've washed
our bedding has been empty

of sleep of any naked kind
of comfort
I want to go back

to when the trees were still
collecting silt

heads trunks bent into the river
   crisp dew

lighting up the spider silk
& my whole self working
       beautifully
I can't
I have watched & watched

the home I loved
a happiness   then a box

migration

sickness has engulfed the swallows
lose everything you are and don't come home
come   take this summer away from me   its birds
are empty and I'm too tired to wash myself

until necessary open arms

running my hand again through my hair in the hospital
heat & sweat in my palm makes it curl so stupidly.
I am not in control
                        of my internal electrics, my spine hell
bent on pounding. my pin-tight bad luck. my fibromyalgia
taking up space in the waiting room spilling
over the seat of a balding pleather armchair
 my doctor tells me *there is nothing much we can do*
& I practice loss outside me. the beginning ache of always
waking very floored.
                reduced workforce, my sympathetic bosses,
dull your trust hard against me. I am never going to work again
the way you want me to. even with my best nodding, this
underlying self.
              this always ill.
                        this month I'll have
to pawn my coats. flowers will make it back & with them
spring.

a sudden move will cause aloud my largely quiet pain
like here I am.

history repeats itself

patterns are trying themselves out in the sky

you could say the sky is showing its teeth
you could say the sky is an unmade bed

      but enough is enough
is exactly what I've had

everything I touch gets sick
you could say that

the beautiful dog lies down at my bedside
the beautiful sky lies down inside my dog
my beautiful unmade dog

how could you

being here is less and less ok

I wake up & confuse it with dying
each day as it comes but with less of what sweetens

I punch my chest purple
drawing pain from everywhere else

last week I went for a run & my knees
   dropped me

new fire from shin to sinew

here comes the rest of my life
shrinking like a muscle out of use

skinny as the ankle of our armchair
locked up with last summer's bees
on their backs at the windowsill

here comes the deep complaint
of next door's dog behind a staircase

the fat warmth of streetlight
through my shutters

my body keeps the birds at altitude
sends the worms up throbbing

what happens is my body asks too much
my life goes in the living room

drops its head

what's wrong with me

I woke up today with an ocean
            on my forehead needles
                      passing through the bands of my biceps

this pain is so bad I am salting a bath for it
                            steeping all day

but nothing I can do will stop the depression
of my heavy frame into our sofa   lara   please try

to picture a whole life   in which
the next words you say to anyone will be the last

      right now I am
watching you put your headphones on
                            fixing your hair

      the bus
            threatening to take you away
to crash at the apex of every corner

it's too hot & you've left your water
      in my hand
it's too wet & the tires have exhausted their tread
    it's every day

fixing my slow unchanging agony
            to your far away breathing
your need to leave the house   you're perfect
   in your dress have a safe journey

11"11

all my good days start with you
      a gap in the rain
hard droplets swallowing themselves back down

all the good selves I've had I wish you could
see them

lined up for the starting gun
running for county   brewing steady dopamine
regulating the movements of their bowels
      carrying the shopping
home from the big sainsbury's unhurt
      let's be real

my sickness has a smell I'm sorry but you know it
here in the tail end of a months-long flare up

I have lost considerable beauty   a stone in muscle
our plants go unwatered   get waxy and thin

fog (two)

obviously this is far from over tell the TV
tell the puffed lips of next door's boiling dog
right here beside the flat pigeon of my self
this summer of pretty grainy asphalt cracked
open stomach puffed like a lychee inside out
tell the wet string holding down my breakfast
the dumb chorus of birds circling the doctor's
office that my health is going to get better
she says it isn't I'm sorry get out

w/

with fibromyalgia with acid
reflux ulcers like burst grapes
with black eyes chronic fatigue
bad hair day hair trigger bowel
with a dirty t-shirt warm tea
easy gag good book with hope
for the pot plants with very sore
scapula lymph nodes up
like sharp berries with cooked
breakfast no sleep hand in
my partner's hand
I am sitting in the garden
        not thinking of you
dying

the apples

are deflating & have fallen

it's your job to not feel taken from
when often & completely I don't work

& because you can be you're so sweet

      only my hands & knees
      only the big stars thrumming
through the bathroom window

there's sugar in the earth
apples committing their disappearing bodies

but enough about the damp grass
the two-tree orchard outside my childhood home

I can't go back

I am sticky in the night   the city
my heart goes off like a gun

the way my muscles can't
      make us dinner

this morning

in the absolute quiet of the morning after
almost dying love is knocking about the fluffy
innards of our waffles kitchen table maple syrup
running rich through lurpak we are so sorry
you could cut the tension with forgiveness
and we do sorry squishy shoulder
and your cheek against it
sorry dog paw   moving chair leg
sorry puffy tear duct raw larynx
sunbeams dappling patches
on bananas 10:45
on the big clock
ben shephard

ulcer

big lip of a bad month or
make it a dumb light peeking through spring leaves
noticeably sunk & deep make it your eyes on me
fresh out the shower small mercies your fingers unknotting
about as many buzzing nerves in my back as can be
blinked through a big drug sleep then morning & wow
the latest disappointment still this eye-ache this tug
slips behind your plaited hair on your pillow my head hurts
but less you miraculous through line you whole heart
bleeding its beat along the springs of our mattress thank you

fog (nine)

lives in oscillation of the breeze
the swollen peak of shade my belly is
making on this park bench

did you want to be someone
different you can't you're here
where my body is wearing

the sugared coat of ibuprofen
the dying hope of trees
carrion bird calls it's ok

for pain to crack an egg
it's ok this is happening

on a sunday my hips benched
chipped iron slats meeting coccyx
knees tucked for easy rocking

      my hot hand up my shirt
for light gastro-intestinal relief
& my disappointed girlfriend
who does not show it

under

life as an act of suppression. anything could happen but nothing does. it is humiliating.

nortriptyline. nortriptyline.

the sound of no one clenching teeth.

remote

walking into this one like
oof. another notch a big old step
towards always like here I endlessly am,
soft dry heat of our flat, making coffee
in the good cups. it's nice.
the way each spasm of flesh
brings on another. a slow regrowth
of weeds in this neighbourhood which holds me
east of almost everything that hurts.

soho square

here comes something different & possible the earth
                                      is covered in blades
the blades are covered in our skin
& although the ways I have to live my life have stretched
like police tape round yours   & my useless stomach
is demanding to be emptied
                          I know you'll come with me
    you'll wait on your phone outside the m&s bathrooms
                                & you'll love me
through the spasms in my gut
      the coming exhaustion
            the flush of blood from my face
        even after that maybe

Acknowledgements

With thanks to *Tentacular Magazine* for featuring some earlier versions of these poems. To Emma Jeremy and Arji Manuelpillai for their advice, and to all the brilliant writers in the Poetry School workshop.

A special thanks to Dom Bennett, whose friendship I'm eternally thankful for. To Josephine, for helping me to find the value of space. To Wayne, whose guidance, generosity and support have been a through line during difficult times. To Patricia and Anthony at Out-Spoken, whose time and patience have meant the world.

And to Lara, most of all, for being there when I fall.

Other titles by Out-Spoken Press

Cane, Corn & Gully • SAFIYA KAMARIA KINSHASA

apricot • KATIE O'PRAY

Mother of Flip-Flops • MUKAHANG LIMBU

Dog Woman • HELEN QUAH

Caviar • SARAH FLETCHER

Somewhere Something is Burning • ALICE FRECKNALL

flinch & air • LAURA JANE LEE

Fetch Your Mother's Heart • LISA LUXX

Seder • ADAM KAMMERLING

54 Questions for the Man Who Sold a Shotgun to My Father JOE CARRICK-VARTY

Lasagne • WAYNE HOLLOWAY-SMITH

Mutton Rolls • ARJI MANUELPILLAI

Contains Mild Peril • FRAN LOCK

Epiphaneia • RICHARD GEORGES

Stage Invasion: Poetry & the Spoken Word Renaissance PETE BEARDER

Nascent • VOL 1: AN ANTHOLOGY

Ways of Coping • OLLIE O'NEILL

The Neighbourhood • HANNAH LOWE

The Games • HARRY JOSEPHINE GILES

Songs My Enemy Taught Me • JOELLE TAYLOR

To Sweeten Bitter • RAYMOND ANTROBUS

Dogtooth • FRAN LOCK

How You Might Know Me • SABRINA MAHFOUZ

Heterogeneous, New & Selected Poems • ANTHONY ANAXAGOROU

Titanic • BRIDGET MINAMORE

Email: press@outspokenldn.com